"ART THEORY
FOR WEB DESIGN

ART THEORY
FOR WEB DESIGN

BY

JENNIFER GOLBECK

Scott/Jones Inc., Publishers

P.O. Box 696 • El Granada, CA 94018
email: scotjones2@aol.com • Fax: 650-726-4693

Art Theory for Web Design

Jennifer Golbeck

Copyright 2005, Scott/Jones, Inc.

ISBN: 1-57676-142-8

The publisher wishes to acknowledge the memory and influence of James F. Leisy. Thanks, Jim. We miss you.

Production Manager:
Mario M. Rodriguez

Copyediting:
Jean Costen

Composition and Text Design:
Lee Anne Dollison

Cover Design:
Jennifer Golbeck

Book Manufacturing:
Phoenix Color

Scott/Jones Publishing Company Editorial Group:
Richard Jones, Denise Simon, Leata Holloway, and Patricia Miyaki

Production Management:
Mario M Rodriguez

Marketing and Sales:
Victoria Judy, Leata Holloway

Business Operations:
Michelle Robelet, Cathy Glenn

Printed in China

A Word About Trademarks

ADDITIONAL TITLES OF INTEREST FROM SCOTT/JONES

Extended Prelude to Programming, Concepts and Design, 2/e
by Stewart Venit

Focus on Excel 2003
by Julie Hayward Spooner

Excel 2003: Volume I, Core Concepts in Excel, 5/e
Excel 2003: Volume II, Advanced Concepts in Excel, 5/e
by Karen Jolly

Starting Out with C++, 4/e
Starting Out with C++ Brief, 4/e
Starting Out with C++ Alternate, 4/e
Starting Out with Java
Starting Out with Java Alternate
Stating Out with Visual Basic.Net, 2/e
by Tony Gaddis

Third Edition
Starting Out with C++,
Third Alternate Edition
by Tony Gaddis

C by Discovery,
Third Edition
by L.S. and Dusty Foster

Assembly Language for the IBM PC Family,
Third Edition
by William Jones

The Visual Basic 6 Coursebook, Fourth Edition
QuickStart to JavaScript
QuickStart to DOS for Windows 9X
by Forest Lin

Advanced Visual Basic.Net,
Third Edition
by Kip Irvine

HTML for Web Developers
Server-Side Programming for Web Developers
by John Avila

The Complete A+ Guide to PC Repair
The Complete Computer Repair Textbook, Third Edition
by Cheryl Schmidt

Windows 2000 Professional Step-by-Step
Windows XP Professional Step-by-Step
by Leslie Hardin and Deborah Tice

The Windows 2000 Professional Textbook
Prelude to Programming: Concepts and Design
The Windows XP Textbook
by Stewart Venit

The Windows 2000 Server Lab Manual
by Gerard Morris

Web Developer Foundations: Using XHTML
Second Edition
by Terry Felke-Morris

ACKNOWLEDGEMENTS

Thanks to my students at the George Washington University who helped me develop and refine this material. Special thanks to Tianhui Cai (Tiffany) for permission to use her web design as an example.

I would especially like to express my gratitude to all of my friends, colleagues, and students who read chapters and made comments on the drafts, including William Cain, Mike Grove, Sora Kim, Jordan Katz, Ruth Matthews, Bijan Parsia, and Robin Zimmer..

A most sincere thanks to the reviewers of this text who provided me with excellent advice for revision: Susan Andrews, Vicki Cox, Richard Hull, Diane Stinson, and Bob Yavits.

Everyone at Scott/Jones Publishing was incredibly supportive of this process. Thanks to everyone there with whom I interacted directly or indirectly.

Most of all, thanks to my husband, Dan Norton, who encouraged me through every step of this process, and to my parents, Irene and John, for their support through every project I've ever done. Finally, thanks to my two dogs, Pi (π) and K, who influenced these chapters in many ways. ■

For Dan

TABLE OF CONTENTS

CHAPTER 1: COLOR FOUNDATIONS FOR ART THEORY

LEARNING OBJECTIVES

- Understand the RGB color system
- Learn to describe colors with 256 values in decimal and hexadecimal
- Introduce the color name system
- Understand the use of web-safe colors

1.1 COLOR MIXING

In elementary school, you probably learned that the three primary colors were red, yellow, and blue, and that other colors are created by mixing those together. For paints, this is absolutely correct. Colors of light combine in different ways than colors of paint. The three primary colors of light are red, green, and blue. If you have ever seen a large projection television, you will notice that the three large lights are red, green, and blue. If you look closely at a computer monitor or a television screen, you will find that each pixel is actually made up of a red, green and blue stripes.

There are two ways to mix colors to form other colors. Additive color mixing uses the red, green, blue set of primary colors, while subtractive color mixing has red, yellow, and blue as primaries. Subtractive color mixing will be discussed in Chapter 2. HTML and Cascading Style Sheets (CSS) use additive color mixing, which is presented here.

Additive color mixing describes how the eye interprets light to perceive color. The three primary colors, red, green, and blue, combine to form the secondary colors cyan (green + blue), yellow (red + green), and magenta (red + blue). This system is called additive because, as colors are combined, the wavelengths and luminosity (brightness) are added together.

The primary colors of light (red, green, and blue) are combined to create any other color, just as the primary colors of paint (red, green, and yellow) are used. Since the red-green-blue system (abbreviated

RGB) deals with colors of light, it is useful to think in terms of percentages. If a light is off, it is at 0% strength, while a light that is all the way on is at 100% strength. There are values in between, when the light may be, for example, at 20% of its brightest value.

Creating colors from the red, green, and blue primaries, is a matter of determining at what power strength each light should be set. Black, of course, is created by having no light of any color. When your monitor or television is off, the screen is black and none of the pixels are lit. White, on the other hand, is made by having full strength of all three primary colors. Shades of gray are created by using equal amounts of red, green, and blue. A mid-toned gray, for example, would be red at 50% strength, green at 50% strength, and blue at 50% strength.

These three primaries combine to form secondary colors in slightly different ways than the colors you used in art class. Red and blue create magenta—a bright purple. Blue and green create cyan, also called teal. Unlike the colors of paint, red and green create yellow. From this basis, we can go on to make other colors as well. For example, orange has more red than yellow has, so in the RGB system, orange is made of some red, less green, and no blue. As another example, bluish-purple would be made of no green, the maximum strength of blue, and a bit less red.

Colors are lightened or darkened much as they would be in art class. Bright yellow, for example, is 100% red, 100% green, and 0% blue. To get a paler yellow in art class, we would mix yellow with white. The same is done in RGB. Since white is 100% of every color, and yellow already has 100% of both red and green, a paler yellow is created by adding blue. A very pale yellow would have lots of blue, say 90%, while a color that is only slightly lighter than the original would have only 10-20% blue. The same applies for all colors. Bright red is 100% red, with no green and blue. To get pink, equal amounts of blue and green are added to move red towards white. One hundred percent red, 50% blue and 50% green make a strong pink. More blue and green, say 90% each, would create a very pale pink.

The general rule for making lighter colors is to take the original pure color, and add in other colors to move toward white (100% of every color). Creating darker colors is exactly the opposite. Since black is made of no red, no green, and no blue, dark versions of a color are made by lowering the values toward 0.

To go from pure red to a dark red color, the green and blue values do not change—they stay at 0. The red value, however, is lowered, thus moving somewhere between a pure red and black. Maroon, for example, is made up of no green, no blue, and about 60% red. A deep

▼ TABLE 1.1: Colors and the corresponding 24-bit color values

Color	Red,Green,Blue	Color	Red,Green,Blue
Red	255,0,0	Black	0,0,0
Blue	0,0,255	White	255,255,255
Green	255,0,0	Orange	255,127,0
Yellow	255,255,0	Purple	127,127,0
Magenta	255,0,255	Pink	255,127,127
Cyan	0,255,255	Gray	127,127,127

purple would be made the same way. The green value would remain at zero, while the red and blue values would both be lowered an equal amount.

1.2 24-BIT COLORS

In HTML, and many other systems, it is very common to use a scale with 256 values each for red, green, and blue. With these different possibilities, an astounding number of colors can be created. For each of the 256 values of red, there are 256 different values of green, for a total of 65,536 red-green combinations. For each of the red-green combinations, there are also 256 different values of blue. This means that there are well over sixteen million different color combinations.

A natural question is why 256? It may seem like an unusual choice. This number is based on the very foundations of how computers work. All data in a computer is encoded in 1s and 0s. This is called the *binary system*, and a single 0 or 1 is called a '*bit*'. Anything the computer deals with is represented by a sequence of bits. For example, using the ASCII system, the character 'a' is actually stored in the computer as '01100001'. Similarly, each color is represented as a sequence of bits. Each color of the red-green-blue sequence is also represented as eight bits (also called a *byte*). For each bit, there are two possible values: 0 or 1. Since there are eight bits, there are 2^8, or 256 possible values for each color. With three composite colors, each represented in 8 bits, each color is made up of a total of 24 bits (8 for red, 8 for green, and 8 for blue). This is called the *24-bit* color system.

With 256 values for each color, 0% is still represented as 0. The highest value, or 100% of a color, is indicated with the number 255. The highest number in the scale is 255 because 0 is included. Since 0 is the first number, 255 is the 256th number.

⁘ 1.3 Hexadecimal Colors

In HTML, color specifications are made as follows:

```
<body bgcolor="#ff6a00">
```

The color in this case, "#ff6a00", does not look like the 24-bit system from above. Examining this value reveals that there are six characters making up the color value. The first two characters are the red value, the third and fourth are the green value, and the last two are the blue. In this case, red has the value "ff", green is "6a", and blue is "00".

Although it looks different, these numbers actually represent the 24-bit system of encoding colors. Since only two characters are used to represent each color, the numbers 0 through 255 cannot be used directly, since numbers over 99 are three characters long and would not fit into the space for two characters. To fit 256 values into only two places, HTML uses the *hexadecimal system*.

Our normal counting system is *base-10*. That means that each digit can hold ten different values: 0-9. The base-10 system is also called the *decimal* system. *Hexadecimal* is base-16. That means each "digit" holds sixteen different values: 0-15. Of course, there has to be some other way to represent 10, 11, 12, 13, 14, and 15 as a single "digit". These are represented by a, b, c, d, e, and f respectively.

Two digits in a base-10 system can represent one hundred different values (0-99). For each of the ten possible values in the first, or leftmost, digit, there are ten different digits that can be in the second, or rightmost, place. In a base-16 system, we can represent 256 values. For each of the sixteen values (0-f) of the first digit, there are sixteen different values for the second digit. We multiply 16 x 16 = 256.

In Table 1.2 on the next page, we see that "10" in hexadecimal actually represents the value 16, and "20" represents 32. Counting this way goes all the way up to "ff" which represents 255.

To write a color into a HTML document, the first step would be to choose the values of each color on the 256-valued scale, and then convert them to their hexadecimal representation. The values for all three colors are combined into a single string, and put into the document.

The proper syntax requires a "#" sign before any hexadecimal color. Generally, current browsers will not have a problem if the "#" is left off, but it should be used just as part of good coding practice. Future web browsers may require us to use this syntax, anyway.

Converting from decimal to hexadecimal becomes easier with practice, and many web designers can actually pick colors directly from the hexadecimal system. Since in most cases we only want an approx-

▼ TABLE 1.2: Some corresponding Decimal and Hexadecimal values

Decimal	Hexadecimal	Decimal	Hexadecimal
1	1	26	1a
2	2	27	1b
3	3	28	1c
4	4	29	1d
5	5	30	1e
6	6	31	1f
7	7	32	20
8	8	33	21
9	9	34	22
10	a	35	23
11	b	36	24
12	c	37	25
13	d	38	26
14	e	39	27
15	f	40	28
16	10	41	29
17	11	42	2a
18	12	43	2b
19	13	44	2c
20	14	45	2d
21	15	46	2e
22	16	47	2f
23	17	48	30
24	18	49	31
25	19	50	32

imate color, this is not a problem. When a very exact color match is required, the conversion can become tedious. There are many places on the web where you can find decimal to hexadecimal converters, including on the website for this book. Many software packages also provide the hexadecimal code for a selected color. Both of these types of tools make using hexadecimal color values easier.

▼ FIGURE 1.1: Color Picker in Adobe(r) Photoshop(r) 7.0

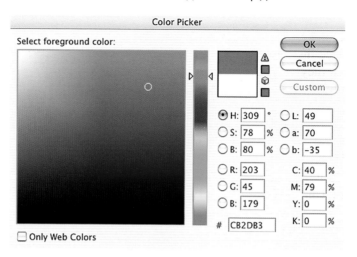

Figure 1.1 shows the Color Picker box in Adobe Photoshop. It shows several different methods for choosing colors, including RGB. It also provides a box that shows the hexadecimal code for each color. Users can choose a color from the palette by moving the vertical slider and clicking in the large box, or entering values into any of the boxes. As the values are adjusted, all of the other values update. For example, if a user were to type "0" into the "R" box, "255" into the G box, and "0" into the "B" box, the hexadecimal field would automatically update to show "00ff00". Users can also type hexadecimal values into that field to directly match colors in graphics to the colors chosen in their HTML documents.

∴ 1.4 COLOR NAMES

In addition to using the hexadecimal system above, HTML also defines sixteen English names that can be used in place of the number code.

▼ TABLE 1.3: HTML and XHTML standard color names with their hexadecimal codes

aqua (#00ffff)	gray (#808080)	navy (#008000)	silver (#c0c0c0)
black (#000000)	green (#008000)	olive (#808000)	teal (#008080)
blue (#0000ff)	lime (#00ff00)	purple (#800080)	yellow (#ffff00)
fuchsia (#ff00ff)	maroon (#800000)	red (#ff0000)	white (#ffffff)

Although not part of the standard, many browsers support an extended color name palette, defined as part of the X Window System. There are hundreds of color names in this palette, such as "lavenderblush3," "whitesmoke," "mistyrose1," and "blanchedalmond." Since these names are not part of the standard, there is no guarantee that they will appear the same across browsers, or even that they will appear close to the expected color. It is always better to use the corresponding hexadecimal code that is guaranteed to work in all browsers.

⋰ 1.5 Web Colors

Using the hexadecimal system, we can create over sixteen million colors. Until the early 2000's, most people had computers that could only display 256 different colors. To further complicate the matter, Macintosh computers and some monitors displayed some of these colors differently than PCs. To take this into account, a set of 216 "web-safe" colors was defined as the color palette that would display the same on all computer platforms. Instead of 256 possible shades of each color, this palette is limited to six shades of red, six of green, and six of blue, for a total of 216 colors. These six values correspond to the hexadecimal codes of 00, 33, 66, 99, cc, and ff. Note that the notion of "web-safe" is not part of any standard, and in fact, some of the color names defined as part of the HTML and XHTML standard are *not* part of the 216 color palette.

If a web page uses a color that is not in the range of colors that a computer can show, the browser either converts it to the closest color in its palette, or dithers the color. *Dithering* replaces the color with

▼ **Figure 1.2:** The two swatches above show the same gradient. The first image has a smooth color transition and uses the full 24-bit color palate. The second image uses the web safe palate and dithers the intermediate colors.

alternating pixels of two different colors. From far away, the two colors seem to blend together to match the original color, but close up, dithered colors look grainy.

The number of people who have this 256-color limit is quickly shrinking. Statistics vary, but in the summer of 2004, these users made up 1-3% of all page accesses. This does not mean, however, that everyone else can see all sixteen million colors. Approximately 30% of web users can only see about 65,500 colors. In this system, called the 16-bit system, there are approximately 40 different values for each of red, green, and blue. Matters are further complicated by the fact that even if you limit yourself to the 216 color web-safe palette, you may still get dithering on 16-bit systems because some of the 216 colors that work on 256 color systems do not properly display on 16-bit systems.

With all this incompatibility, you may be wondering what to do. The answer depends on the purpose of your website and who the target audience is. The type of computers your audience uses can vary widely. If you are targeting high-end graphics designers, there is a good chance that all of them will have systems that can see all 16 million colors. If you are designing for a more general audience, then you will need to consider whether to trade-off effects in your graphics for identical performance across systems, or you must be willing to accept that some systems will not display your pages as well as others. The best course of action, regardless of your choice, is to always check your pages on a variety of computers using different browsers and different settings. This will let you see how the page looks in several different configurations, and your choices about color can be more informed.

∴ 1.6 COLORS IN CASCADING STYLE SHEETS

Many CSS properties, such as "color" and "background-color", require colors as values. Hexadecimal values can be used, provided they are prefaced with a "#". A variant of the HTML hexadecimal system is also available in CSS. Recall that the value for red, green, and blue in each color occupies two positions of the hexadecimal code. If, for each color, the two positions contain the same character, a three-character hexadecimal value can be used in its place. This three-position value just has the one character used for each color. For example, the hexadecimal "#ff99cc" could be written as "#f9c" in CSS. The value "#1177dd" can be written "#17d".

The basic color names are also valid values in CSS. On top of this, a function can be used to create colors. This function works much like a function you may have written in algebra class. The name of this function is "rgb" and three arguments are passed to it. The first represents the red value, the second represents green, and the third represents blue. The values can be given on a scale of 0-255 or in percentages.

```
rgb(255,255,255)
rgb(100%,50%,25%)
```

∴ 1.7 Review

- Red, green, and blue are the three primary colors of light, which uses additive color mixing.
- These three colors can be combined to form any other colors.
- The *24-bit* color scale has 256 different values of red, 256 values of blue, and 256 values of green
- In the 24-bit system, there are over sixteen million color combinations.
- HTML uses the *hexadecimal* system for representing 24-bit colors.
- In the hexadecimal system, there are sixteen values of each digit, represented as 0-9, followed by a-f to represent the values 10-15.
- Colors in HTML are prefixed with "#" and written as a series of six characters. The first two characters contain the red value, the third and fourth contain the green value, and the last two contain the blue value.
- On older computer systems, a limited number of colors can be displayed.
- The "web-safe" color palette contains 216 colors that will properly display on systems that can only show 256 colors.

∴ 1.8 Questions

1. Define the following terms:
   a. Base-16
   b. Hexadecimal
   c. Additive color mixing
   d. RGB
   e. 24-bit color
   f. Web safe palate
   g. HTML color name
   h. Dithering
   i. Bit
   j. Primary color
2. Fill in the blank.
   a. The three primary colors of light are _____, _____, and _____.
   b. The hexadecimal system uses base-_____ numbers.

   c. With _____ bits, over sixteen million colors can be created.

   d. The RGB system uses _____ color mixing.

   e. Hexadecimal values use the digits 0-9, and _____ - _____ to represent the value from 10-15.

   f. The hexadecimal code for pure red is #_____.

   g. _____ describes the practice of using combinations of colors to give the illusion of a color that is not in the palate.

   h. There are _____ colors in the web safe palate.

   i. _____ percentage of users are restricted to seeing only colors in the web safe palate.

   j. In order to create a light blue color, full strength blue is combined with lower values of _____ and _____.

3. True or False:

   a. In the RGB system, yellow and blue mix to create green.

   b. The color names that are part of the HTML standard are a subset of the web safe palate.

   c. If a color is not part of the web safe palate, it will appear dithered on *most users computers.*

   d. Hexadecimal colors are represented with a base-10 scale.

   e. In the RGB system, blue is a primary color.

   f. The web safe palate uses 256 values of red, green, and blue.

   g. The same hexadecimal system used in HTML can also be used to create color in CSS.

   h. The color names "lavenderblush3," "whitesmoke," and "mistyrose1" are part of the HTML standard color names.

   i. The "#" character is used as a prefix for hexadecimal colors.

   j. #f0i3a7 is a valid hexadecimal color.

4. In an RGB system, what combination of the primary colors produces the following colors:

   a. Purple

   b. Yellow

   c. Red

   d. Orange

   e. Black

   f. Blue

   g. Green

   h. Pink

   i. White

   j. Gray

5. Consider the format and encoding of numbers in the hexadecimal system.

   a. How many characters/digits are used for each color?

   b. How many different values are there for each primary color?

   c. How many total characters are used to define a hexadecimal color?

    d. In what order are the primary color values listed in a hexadecimal color (e.g. what color is defined first, second, and then third)?

    e. How many total colors can be produced in the hexadecimal system?

6. Consider color names.

    a. How many color names are part of the HTML and XHTML standard?

    b. Go online and see how many *other* color names you can find. How many are there (approximate if the number is large) and what organization(s) proposes those color names?

    c. Should non-standard color names be used in HTML documents? Why or why not?

7. Convert the following numbers to the corresponding two-digit hexadecimal codes

    a. 43

    c. 32

    d. 176

    e. 0

    f. 50

    g. 99

    h. 255

    i. 128

    j. 160

8. Convert the following two-digit hexadecimal codes to base-10 numbers (e.g. 0f in hexadecimal is 15 in base-10)

    a. 10

    b. a0

    c. 6f

    d. ad

    e. b4

    f. 7e

    g. 9c

    h. 23

    i. e2

    j. 81

9. Consider web-safe colors.

    a. What are web-safe colors?

    b. What happens when a color that is not web-safe is viewed on an older computer?

    c. How many colors are in the web-safe palette?

    d. The web safe palate was designed to accommodate users with how many colors on their monitors?

∴ **1.9 EXERCISES**

1. Create a web page that sets the following attributes using the hexa-decimal color system. Use the proper attributes in the `<body>` tag.
   a. background color
   b. text color
   c. active link
   d. visited link
   e. unvisited link
2. Repeat exercise 1 using the appropriate CSS properties in place of the HTML attributes.
3. Project A: Create the content for a website with at least 5 pages.
   a. Use an external style sheet to specify the colors of elements and any background images so that the design for the website can be easily changed.
   b. This stage of Project A should focus mainly on developing content. The design will be refined in future chapters.

CHAPTER 2: COLOR THEORY

LEARNING OBJECTIVES

- Describe the basic principles and terminology of color mixing.

- Introduce color schemas and understand the aesthetics of color composition.

- Demonstrate how to apply the doctrines of color theory to web design

As we now know, HTML uses a Red-Green-Blue system for making colors. Artistic color combinations (called subtractive color mixing), with which most of us are familiar, have a Red-Yellow-Blue base, and these form the basics of color theory. The theories of combining colors discussed here will apply, regardless of the system you use to create the colors. With this theory, you can make choices about design and composition, after which you can create the correct shades in the RGB system.

2.1 THE 12-HUE COLOR WHEEL

The image of the color wheel is probably familiar to most of us from elementary school art classes. Understanding the relationships among these colors makes up the foundation of color theory.

▼ FIGURE 2.1: The 12-hue Color Wheel

Each of the colors on the wheel differs by *hue*. Scientifically, hue is the quality of a color determined by its dominant wavelength. Violet has the shortest wavelength and red has the longest. In easier terms, hue is the chromaticity, or the basic difference between colors with which we are all familiar. Red is a different color than orange. Both are different from green or blue.

The first principle to understand is color mixing. Red, yellow and blue are the three primary colors, and are shown in a triangle in the center of the wheel. These are the base colors, which cannot be created from any others. Combining these colors makes the three secondary colors: equal amounts of blue and yellow make green, yellow and red make orange, and red and blue make violet. These combinations are probably very familiar. In the 12-hue color wheel, each of the primary and secondary colors appear on the edges of the color wheel, and between them are the intermediate or "tertiary" colors. Intermediate colors are made by combining a primary and secondary color. These are named with the primary color first: yellow-orange, red-orange, red-violet, blue-violet, blue-green, and yellow-green. The difference between these colors is called hue. Obviously, many millions of other colors can be created with various combinations of these, but the twelve on this scale are effective in describing the basics of color theory and showing how to combine colors for effective design.

⠶ 2.2 SATURATION AND COLOR VALUES

Many additional colors can be made from a single hue. On the color wheel, each color is at full saturation. *Saturation* refers to the intensity or vividness of a color. At full saturation, a color is at its purest

▼ FIGURE 2.2: Six different saturations of red

▼ FIGURE 2.3: A 12 Color Gray Scale

▼ FIGURE 2.4: Tints and Shades

Tints of Red   *Shades of Red*

value. It is not diluted in any way. As saturation decreases, colors fade to gray.

Grays have no hue saturation, and are called neutral colors. Since there is no hue to grays, they are differentiated by their brightness. This light-dark difference makes different values of a color. In Figure 2.3, the center gray is completely neutral, half way between black and white. Six lighter values and six darker values are shown, equally spaced to white and black. Values that are lighter than the middle value are called "tints" of gray, and darker values are called "shades" of gray.

Values do not just apply to neutral colors. Any hue of any saturation can also be combined with whites and blacks to produce tints and shades of that color.

The figure below shows the twelve different hues of the color wheel with the twelve equidistant steps from black to white shown above.

▼ FIGURE 2.5: Equally spaced values of twelve hues

What is very interesting from this figure is that pure yellow occurs four steps from white, while pure orange is six steps, pure red is eight, and pure violet is ten steps down. This tells us that colors, in addition to having their own hues, also reach their purest values at different light and dark values. Pure yellow is a lighter color than pure violet. When combining colors, this difference is important: to have a brilliant and intense yellow, it can be placed against other light colors and look very intense. There is no brilliant dark shade of yellow, which is important to consider if a dark composition is being considered. The same applies for violet, which is intense in the darker shades, but is rather dull in lighter tints.

⁚• **2.3 COLOR COMPOSITION**

Now that we have a basic understanding of the terminology of colors, we will study ways to combine them, and the effects that will have. In this section, we present five color schemas. Schemas are guidelines for combining colors in interesting and aesthetically pleasing ways. In the next section, we will see how to apply these schemas to web page design.

2.3.1 Monochromatic Schemas

The monochromatic schema (*mono* means "one" and *chromatic* means "color") uses different values of one hue to make an image. Clearly, only a single value of a single color would not make for an interesting image—it would just be a solid blob. When creating a monochromatic composition, there is more freedom than that. One color is chosen, and the image is made from varying values (tints and shades), and saturations of that color. The painting below, for example, is a monochromatic image made up of many different types of blue.

▼ FIGURE 2.6: A monochromatic image in shades and tints of blue.

▼ FIGURE 2.7: Pairs of complimentary colors on the color wheel, and the painting done in complimentary blue and orange values.

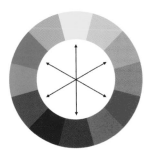

2.3.2 Complimentary Colors

Complimentary colors are found directly across from one another on the color wheel. Blue and orange are complimentary; so are violet and yellow, red and green. Complimentary colors have the greatest contrast of any color pairs. Notice that each pair has one primary color and one secondary color that is made up of the other two primaries. If you mix any two complimentary colors, it produces a neutral grayish-brown.

When presented with a single color, the human eye naturally seeks the compliment. If you place a gray square on an orange field, the square will appear to take on a bluish hue. Similarly, as an experiment, try wearing a pair of yellow-lens sunglasses for half an hour. When you take them off, you will notice a violet tint to the real world. This is because your eye has been "filling in" violet while you were looking through the yellow, and it takes a few minutes to readjust after removing the glasses. This effect means that compositions that use complimentary colors appear very stable.

As with the monochromatic schema, a complimentary schema does not mean that only two colors are used. Two hues are chosen, say orange and blue. Then, different saturations and values of those two colors are chosen. One of the two colors can be emphasized by using at a high saturation and close to its pure value while the other color is used at a lower saturation or at a shade/tint distant from its purest value.

2.3.3 Analogous Colors

Analogous colors are any set of three to five colors found consecutively on the color wheel. Because they are all so close, they provide little contrast to one another. They also make for very elegant compositions.

▼ FIGURE 2.8: A group of analogous colors on the color wheel and the painting composed of those same analogous colors.

Using the same techniques described for complimentary colors, one or two colors can be emphasized by using them at higher intensity. A composition that uses two main colors, such as green and orange, can be tied together by adding variants of the intermediate hues on the color wheel. A pale yellow background and some yellow-orange and yellow-green highlights, as is shown in Figure 2.8, will bring the otherwise contrasting colors together.

2.3.4 Warm and Cool

The color wheel is divided in half, separating "warm" colors from "cool" colors. Warm colors are yellows, oranges, and reds (like those found in fire and the sun) while the cool colors are violets, blues, and greens (those found in water and ice). Red-orange is the warmest while blue-green (it's direct opposite) is the coolest.

▼ FIGURE 2.9: The warm colors of the spectrum and the painting done in highly saturated warm colors..

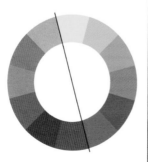 

▼ FIGURE 2.10: The cool colors of the spectrum and the painting done in highly saturated cool colors.

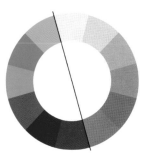 

While it may seem odd to associate temperature with colors, some interesting physiological effects back this up. Experiments have shown that people in rooms painted blue-green perceive the temperature to be colder than people in the same temperature room painted red-orange. There is, in fact, a research community that studies the psychological and physiological effects of color. This dictates everything from tablecloth colors in restaurants (red tends to make people feel more hungry) to wall colors in hospitals (green is calming).

In composition, warm colors appear closer to the viewer while cool colors seem farther away, fading into the background.

2.3.5 Harmonic Colors and Triads

Harmonic colors are equally spaced on the color wheel. Complimentary colors are one type of harmonic color set, called harmonic dyads.

▼ FIGURE 2.11: A triad selection on the color wheel (blue-violet, yellow-green, and red-orange) and the painting composed of values of those three colors.

Harmonic triads, a collection of three colors, are another. A harmonic triad is created by selecting three equidistant colors on the color wheel. This can be visualized by placing an equilateral triangle in the center of the color wheel and choosing the three colors at the points of the triangle. Red, blue, and yellow make up the strongest of these triads. The secondary colors, orange, violet, and green, make up another. Any of the four different harmonic triads will work well together in composition.

⁂ 2.4 COLOR THEORY IN WEB DESIGN

2.4.1 Color Composition on Web Pages

Composition is much more than just putting colors together. It involves layout, use of space, flow, and lines. Most of those issues will be addressed in Chapter 3, and in this chapter we will focus exclusively on the composition of color.

All of the schemas we learned in the previous section are applicable to page design as well as to paintings. The choice of colors for web pages, in fact, will be one of the most noticeable effects on the look and feel of your website. Thus, it is important to consider which combination of colors will be best. Hue is very important, but also consider issues of light and dark, and saturation.

Consider the six examples on the following page. Each implements one of the schemas presented above. They all show the same web page, with the same images, layout, and text, but the feel of each is very different simply due to the color combinations.

Of course, there are countless variations within each theme, but these examples give a clear sense of the dramatic difference color makes. Compare the feel from each design. Looking at the last two, notice how the warm schema really looks warmer and has a cozier feel, while the cool schema is in more relaxing tones. The pages done in harmonic triad and complementary colors both each show more contrast than any of the other four pages.

The above examples also give some idea about where color elements can occur in your website. Backgrounds, text and link colors, icons, and images in the site can all be united in a coherent theme by using a color schema. Start by choosing a color schema and defining the elements in your website. As you select colors for the graphical elements, try several different combinations to find which looks best. Remember also that unvisited, visited, and active link colors should all tie in with the color scheme.

▼ FIGURE 2.12: The same web page in six different color schemas

Monochromatic in Blue

Analogous Schema (red, red-violet, violet, and blue-violet)

Complimentary Schema

Harmonic Triad (violet, green, and orange)

Warm Schema

Cool Schema

Chances are that your website will be designed to present information, not to simply exist as a work of art. This being the case, it is important to consider some usability issues when selecting which colors to use in what values on each part of your web page.

▼ FIGURE 2.13: Color on Color examples

2.4.2 Text and Backgrounds

Most of the color theory discussion in the previous sections talked about the principles of combining different hues. When designing web pages, it is important to consider issues of light and dark as well.

When adding a background, the most important factor to consider is readability. Bright red text on a bright blue background is simply not legible. For text to be readable, there must be a large difference in the light and dark values of the foreground and background. Since

▼ FIGURE 2.14: Both of these screen captures show white and black text over a striped background. Notice that it is difficult to read text in either color. For both images, the light colored stripe in the background is only 20% lighter than the dark color, but this still makes the text difficult to read because of the changing contrast.

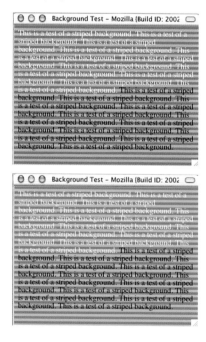

▼ FIGURE 2.15: A light background with little light-dark contrast makes our document with black text much more readable.

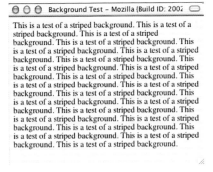

most of us are used to it, dark text on a light background works best. While black and white is always a safe bet, very light tints of a color combined with dark shades of a color (as shown in the web site examples above) can also be effective.

We need to be even more careful when selecting a background pattern. Generally, it is a good idea to stick with solid colors for your background. Images can be used in this capacity to introduce, say, a solid bar of one color along the right side of the page while leaving a different solid color behind the main content. Used properly, background images can add a subtle and elegant touch to a page.

If you must place a repeating pattern across the page, there are a few options. First, consider using a background image overlaid with a solid background for the text. This will keep your text legible while still introducing the effect. If ypu are going to use a background image alone, it is important to look for several features.

1. Within an image, there should be very little contrast in hue or in light-dark. If an image uses several different hues, text may be easy to read over one color and difficult to read over another. With even a relatively small difference in light-dark values, text can become very difficult to read. Figure 2.14 illustrates this on a striped background.

   The striped effect can still be achieved. Figure 2.15 shows the same document with a striped background. Here, there is only a 5% difference in the values of the green, and we have chosen to use light values instead of the middle range values in Figure 2.14. The black text is very legible here, and the subtle striping effect is still achieved.

▼ FIGURE 2.16: A background in legible colors but with bad tiling makes this text difficult to read. The sharp light-dark contrast at the seams forces users to re-adjust their eyes to focus on the text.

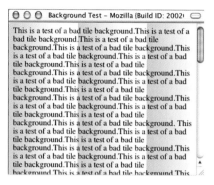

2. The image should tile well. There should be no visible seams as the image repeats—this line will distract your user from the text. Many free background images that tile well are available online. Figure 2.16 shows how seams can interrupt the text.
3. If there is a pattern in the image, it should be small (a few pixels) so it does not disrupt the readability of the text. Large patterns, like big checkerboard layouts or recognizable icons or pictures, stick out from the background and overwhelm the text, as shown in Figure 2.17.

▼ FIGURE 2.17: A large pattern in the background makes this text difficult to read. While the black letters are legible over any of the individual colors, the changing shades are distracting and make the user work harder to see what is actually written.

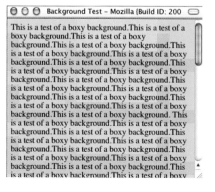

⠂⠂ 2.5 REVIEW

- Red, blue, and yellow are the three *primary colors* in subtractive color mixing, such as is done with paints.
- Combining primary colors makes the three *secondary colors*: green, orange, and violet.
- Mixing a secondary color and a primary color produces a *tertiary color.*
- The difference between these colors is a difference in *hue*.
- *Saturation* refers to the intensity of a color. As a color's saturation decreases, it fades to gray.
- *Values* of a color are made by lightening or darkening it. *Tints* are the lighter values of a color and shades are the darker values.
- *Color Schemas* are different ways to combine colors.
- *Monochromatic schemas* use different values and saturations of a single color.
- *Complimentary colors* are found directly opposite one another on the color wheel.
- *Harmonic triads* are formed by combining three colors that are equidistant on the color wheel.
- *Warm colors* are shades of reds, yellows, and oranges.
- *Cool colors* are shades of blues, greens, and violets.
- For text to be legible, there should be a high light-dark contrast between the background and the foreground.
- When using background images, be sure to preserve light-dark contrast, avoid obvious seams in a tiled image, and use only small patterns to preserve legibility.

⠂⠂ 2.6 QUESTIONS

1. Define the following terms:
   a. Hue
   b. Tint
   c. Shade
   d. Saturation
   e. Contrast
   f. Harmonic Triad
   g. Neutral
   h. Monochromatic
   i. Tertiary color
   j. Subtractive color mixing
2. Fill in the blank:
   a. Green, _____, and _____ make up a harmonic triad.

    b. Red-violet and _____ are complimentary colors.

    c. Green, blue, and violet are _____ colors.

    d. Pink is a _____ of red.

    e. Orange, green, and violet are the three _____ colors.

    f. Warm colors, monochromatic, and analogous are three examples of _____.

    g. An analogous color schema has low _____ among the hues.

    h. _____ is the number of colors in the warm color schema.

    i. _____ is the dominant color schema in figure 2.ex1.

    j. In figure 2.ex1, the dominant colors are _____.

    Figure 2. ex1

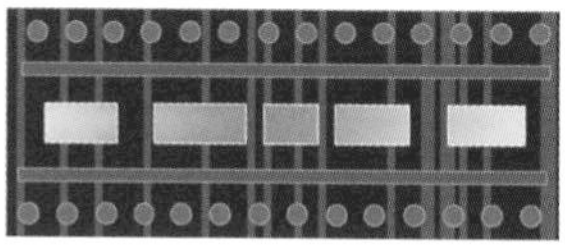

3. True or false:

    a. Red, green, and blue are the primary colors in subtractive color mixing (e.g. when mixing paints).

    b. Red and blue are complimentary colors.

    c. When creating an image with a monochromatic schema, gray, black, and white can only be used if the entire image is in black and white (i.e. there are no saturated hues).

    d. Red, yellow, and blue make up a harmonic triad.

    e. Figure 2.ex2 shows only tints of blue.

    Figure 2. ex2

    f. In subtractive color mixing, green is a primary color.

    g. When naming tertiary colors, the name of the primary color comes first.

    h. Shades of gray can not be used in an image with a monochromatic orange color schema.

    i. Saturation refers to how light (close to white) or dark (close to black) a color is.

    j. A harmonic triad uses 3-5 colors.

4. List all of the colors in each of the following categories:

    a. Primary

    b. Secondary

    c. Tertiary

5. What is a color schema?

6. What does the value of a color describe?

7. List the six tertiary colors.

8. Give an example of the following:
   a. A pair of complimentary colors
   b. A harmonic triad
   c. Three cool colors
   d. Three warm colors
   e. Three analogous colors that include at least once warm and one cool color
9. For terms in Question 1 a-d, show a variant of violet and tell how it relates to the concept. For example, a very pale violet would be an example of a light tint.
10. a. Describe two features of a background that make it difficult to read the overlaying text.
   b. Create an image that is example of each of the features you mentioned in part a.
   c. Create a variant of the images from part b that correct the problem and make the images work well as backgrounds.
11. Using the websites in Figure 2.12, answer the following questions.
   a. Which combinations do you like best? Why?
   b. Do you think adjusting the way a particular schema is used in the websites would change your opinion? For example, if the complimentary schema reversed the violet and yellow, would that improve it? What if it were done in red and green values instead of violet and yellow values?
12. Is there a particular subject matter you think should represented with a particular schema? For example, do you think a medical website should be done in cool colors? Warm colors? Why?
13. Choose two colorsthat are *not* black or white—that will work as a text color and background color. Explain your choices.

∴ **2.7** EXERCISES

1. Choose a topic (it can be about yourself, a company, an organization, or a hobby) and make a homepage about it. Format the text with line breaks, some heading tags (h1, h2, etc), and a few links. Then, set background colors (and/or a background image), link colors, text color, and any images you use in the document to use the following color schemas:
   a. Warm colors
   b. Cool colors
   c. Analogous colors
   d. Complimentary colors
   e. A harmonic triad (think about which three colors make up the triad)
   f. A monochromatic schema

2. Find an image online that you like. Using a photo editor, create a version of the picture that fits into one of the following color schemas:

a. Warm colors

b. Cool colors

c. Analogous colors

d. Complimentary colors

e. A harmonic triad (think about which three colors make up the triad)

f. A monochromatic schema

3. Project A: Choose a color schema and the colors within that schema for the site you started creating as part of Project A.

a. Adjust the style sheet to use the colors you chose.

b. Consider selecting colors within the schema for the following elements

i. Body background and text color

ii. Headings (<h1> through <h6> tags)

iii. Links in all states

iv. Background colors or images for sections of text

v. Image borders

vi. Background colors for form elements and text colors in form elements. If your skills are more advanced, you can use different colors for form fields in focus and out of focus. Figure 2.ex3 shows a form from http://dogster.com that uses color in this way. The active field has an orange background, while the inactive fields have a blue-teal background.

Figure 2. ex3

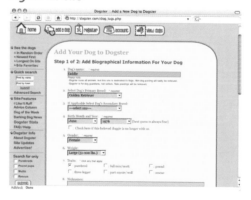

CHAPTER 3: GRAPHIC DESIGN THEORY

LEARNING OBJECTIVES

- Learn the basic elements and principles of design.

- Understand how these design formalisms are combined to produce different effects.

- See how these design examples are used in artwork and web pages.

- Practice implementing this artistic design into web page design.

Color Theory, as described in the previous chapter, presents methods of composing color in aesthetic ways as a basis for web design. Graphic design theory, a broader concept that encompasses the major aspects of composition, is equally useful as a foundation for page layout and design. This chapter will introduce the major elements of design theory with some examples, and present ways that they can be used in web page design.

3.1 ELEMENTS OF DESIGN

3.1.1 Line

Intuitively, we all know what a line is. It is a mark that connects two points. Lines can have different lengths and widths. They can be straight or curved. Depending on the orientation, lines can convey different meaning. Horizontal lines tend to convey a mood of calmness, while vertical lines give a feeling of balance and stability. Diagonal lines give the impression of action or movement.

A focus on direction can help give order to the work, be it a painting or a web page. A page with dominating lines going in all directions will appear chaotic. By using one dominant direction of line, the page will look more unified and stable. Figure 3.1 shows the different effects that line direction can have on the appearance of an object.

▼ **Figure 3.1:** These images of a dragonfly are created using different directions of line. Notice the difference in feeling among the images.

Lines can also be used to give the impression of extending the space that the viewer can see. The Mondrian painting, "Composition with Red, Yellow and Blue," (see Appendix B) uses this technique. The lines give the impression of extending beyond the edges of the canvas.

3.1.2 Shape

A shape is any enclosed or defined area. Contrary to lines, which give a feeling of continuity and movement, shapes are solid and define regions of space. Shapes can be geometric or organic. The primary geometric shapes are squares, circles, and triangles. Squares (and rectangles) are stable and can ground a design. Circles can suggest movement—like a wheel or globe. Triangles and polygons are dynamic and suggest movement. They can be used to emphasize different parts of a page and can create movement with their angles. Organic shapes are irregular and can be anything from the shape of a leaf to a blob. Figure 3.2 shows collections of both geometric and organic shapes.

▼ **Figure 3.2:** The column on the left shows collections of geometric shapes that are both empty and filled in. The column on the right has examples of some organic shapes.

▼ FIGURE 3.3: The first picture shows the Earth in space. The Earth is the foreground, and thus the positive space. The second image shows the positive and negative space. All of the positive space is shown in white and the negative space is shown in black.

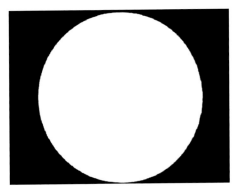

3.1.3 Positive and Negative Space

Positive and negative space work together to define an image. Positive space refers to the foreground or the subject of an image. Negative space is the background or the space around the subject.

The positive space has the shape of the subjects. The shape of the negative space is defined by the shape of the positive space. Once the subjects of the image are removed, the shape of the negative space is revealed.

The print "Mosaic II" by M.C. Escher (See Appendix B) confuses positive and negative space. The white figures could be the foreground, or the black figures could be. Because we are drawn to see one color as the foreground, instead of just seeing a collection of interconnected creatures, the image is confusing and interesting.

▼ FIGURE 3.4: Grass and leaves create a strong visual texture in the left image, while soft circles create a gentle texture in the right one.

3.1.4 Texture

Texture is the feel of a surface. In physical art, the canvas, paper, or other base can create texture, as well as the height and application of the paint or other medium. Obviously, texture cannot be created physically on a web page. In this two-dimensional space, visually created textures can give depth and interest to a design, just as physical textures do three-dimensionally.

Texture in web pages can be used in backgrounds, as elements in the banners and navigation bars, or as decorative elements on the page. When most pages are just flat blocks of color and text, texture can be a dramatic element on a page. Tiled backgrounds are one way that designers can add texture to a page.

3.2 PRINCIPLES OF DESIGN

3.2.1 Movement

In design, movement does not in any way relate to animation. Movement in design is the *suggestion* of motion. Though static pictures cannot move, the idea of movement can be achieved in many ways. If items in the image lean or move in a direction, it may make the view feel like there is about to be some movement on the part of the elements. Multiple stages in movement may also be used to convey motion over time to the viewer. Duchamp's "Nude Descending A Staircase" (see Appendix B) is a prime example of this technique, showing the female subject through several stages of her descent. Optical illusions can also illustrate movement by tricking the eye into seeing it. Figure 3.5 is one such illusion. Even though the image is static, it appears that the circles rotate a bit as you move your eyes.

▼ FIGURE 3.5: An optical illusion that seems to show movement in the image.

Though illusions are fascinating and fun, they are also somewhat disconcerting for the viewer and are not recommend as a web design feature. Other methods of adding movement, however, can create visual interest on a page.

3.2.2 Balance

Imagine each element on the page having a weight. Balance is the principle that describes where that weight is centered. Large elements have more weight than smaller ones. Darker or more vibrant color has more weight than paler or lighter colors, so a small intense block of color will be balanced by a larger, grayish block.

There are two ways to balance a composition. Symmetrical balance is more formal. It has elements equally weighted on either side of the center. Because both sides of the image are weighted evenly, it feels more orderly and stable.

Asymmetrical balance is more chaotic and can create tension in an image. Asymmetry may arise in images that are symmetrically laid out because the elements have different weights. Similarly, graphics with asymmetrically placed elements can be symmetrically balanced because of the weight of the objects.

Consider Figure 3.6. The top row shows two symmetrically balanced images, while the bottom row has two asymmetrically balanced variants. The image in the top left is laid out symmetrically—if the image were cut down the middle, the left and right sides would contain the same elements as mirror images. Since the weight of each side is equal, the image is also symmetrically balanced. Underneath it, in the lower left, is an asymmetrically balanced variant. Although the number and placement of elements has not changed, the weight of the circles on the right has changed. This makes the left side of the image feel heavier. On the right are two versions of an image that has an asymmetric layout. In both, the large gray circle with an inner black circle fills up most of the left hand side and extends past the center of the image onto the right side. The column of small circles only takes up a fraction of the space remaining in the image. The top image still manages to feel balanced, though. This is because the weight of the solid black circles is about the same as the larger gray circle. The lower image is clearly unbalanced. The large filled circle is much heavier than the small open circles on the right, so the image feels heavier on the left.

Consider the content of your website and the audience when playing with balance. If the pages need to be formal, a symmetric balance is the way to go. If the site allows for more visual experimentation, asymmetric balance can be useful and interesting.

▼ FIGURE 3.6: Using the same basic elements, these graphics show how symmetric and asymmetric balance can be created with both symmetric and asymmetric layouts.

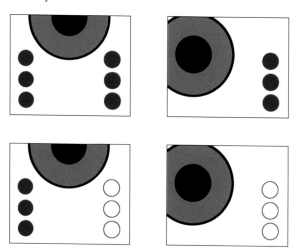

▼ FIGURE 3.7: Different types of rhythm are shown in these four images. The top left is a basic, simple repetition of a single element. The top right shows a rhythm that alternates among four lines. In the lower left is an image with predictable spacing between the lines. The distance doubles between each set of lines as they move away from the center line. The lower right image, though, has no apparent pattern to its repetition, so it is considered irregular or chaotic rhythm.

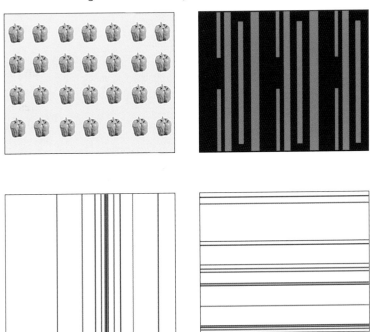

3.2.3 Rhythm

Just as in music, rhythm is created by the repetition of elements. When the same element is repeated over and over, it produces a regular and symmetric visual rhythm. Alternation is another type of rhythm where a sequence of elements are repeated in turn. A predictable pattern of spacing between elements, even the amount of the spacing varies, can also create a regular rhythm. Chaotic rhythm arises when an element or elements are repeated with no apparent pattern to the viewer.

Rhythm can be used to move the viewer's eye across a page. If it is visually clear how the page progresses, readers will have clues about where to start reading and where to go. When the arrangement of text and graphics does not seem to follow a regular, predictable pattern, users will have a difficult time deciding where the content begins and how it flows.

▼ FIGURE 3.8: The use of shape and color emphasizes the circle in this strip of squares.

3.2.4 Emphasis

Emphasis refers to the point or points in the image that most strongly draw the user's attention. Emphasis can be created with many different elements. Color is one common way of creating emphasis, by marking text or a region differently from the rest. Changes in shape, color, size, or light/dark value can also create emphasis. Any regular rhythm with a predictable flow can be used to emphasize an element that interrupts that flow.

⋰ 3.2 GRAPHIC DESIGN THEORY IN WEB DESIGN

As with color theory, the elements presented above can help provide direction in how to design web pages. Each of the paintings in Appendix B illustrates one major design element, but the composition as a whole contains many aspects of design and color theory. Deciding how to combine these elements in a web design page is the foundation of an artistically well designed page.

The design in Figure 3.9 uses line as the dominant element. The lines dividing the sections of the page are one element. The alignment and spacing of the text also creates the appearance of five individual text lines, rather than a block paragraph. There is also diagonal movement in the page. The heading text is aligned on the left. Each line of body text is subsequently indented, and the large text at the bottom aligns on the right. This rhythm where each element moves predictably and regularly toward the right encourages the reader to start at the top and move down across the lines of text. Together, these lines of text form something like a triangle, rooted in the upper right corner of the content space. This creates an asymmetric balance, with more weight on the right hand side.

Figure 3.10 uses shape as the primary element. Each piece of text or heading is displayed on its own shape. Even the decoration at the bottom is a collection of shapes. Comparing this design to the previous one, it is clear to see the difference between the flow of line and the block of the shapes. This design is also strongly center balanced. The heading is centered, the two blocks of text are in the center of

▼ FIGURE 3.9: A page design based on the use of line. Notice the similarities to the work by Mondrian.

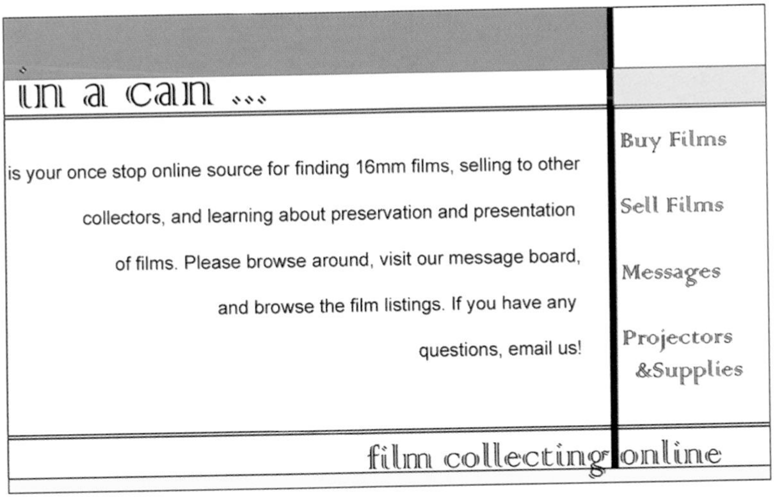

their respective gray rectangles. Those shapes each take up the same width, dividing the page down the middle. The text for the navigation bar is centered on the dark gray strip. Finally, the decorative strip is centered on the bottom. All of the rows of elements fill the same width of the page. The result is that the page looks rooted in the center. Again, the elements of this page—rectangles, text, and background—can be colored according to any of the color schemas already discussed.

▼ FIGURE 3.10: The use of shape as the basic element for page design.

▼ FIGURE 3.11: Emphasis and balance in a page design

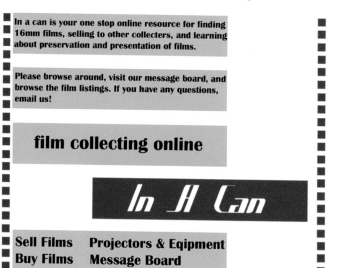

This example in Figure 3.11 uses emphasis and asymmetric balance to create tension in the design. The small black squares evenly frame the image. The gray rectangles with the content are aligned to the left with the large black rectangle slightly offset. This alignment of gray shapes creates a left heavy balance in the image. Visual emphasis is given to the title of the page by the offset and by the color of the negative space (black instead of gray), breaking up the rhythm of the otherwise regular patterns on the page.

Finally, the last example is shown in Figure 3.12. The rectangles, starting with the light vertical one on the left, rotate around to the banner across the top. This is a prime example of movement through multiple views. The blocks of text are aligned to mimic the movement by following the curve of the motion. The navigation elements on the bottom of the page span the same width as the rectangles used in the banner movement. The first link is in the moving rectangles, and the last aligns with the edge of the banner at the top. These elements give cohesion to the page and also establish a rhythm across the bottom. Finally, the circular film reel grounds the image. It adds balance to the page by giving weight to the right side. Even though it is circular, while all of the other elements are rectangular, it is not out of place. The motion of the rectangles is circular, as though they are pivoting along the edge of a circle. The font used in the page title is also composed of perfect circles—notice the shape of the "C" and the "a". These circular elements connect to the shape of the reel.

▼ FIGURE 3.12: The use of movement in a well balanced page.

These are just a few examples illustrating the elements and principles of graphic design. These principles can be found in many well designed pages, as well as in artwork. Studying these features in art can help develop your skill in applying them in your own designs. Modern art, particularly abstract art, can often provide inspiration for designing pages because the design features are more apparent. Interesting uses of line, shape, and emphasis can be carried over into the design of web pages. Advertising and print media are also excellent examples. Your local bookstore will have a full section dedicated to graphic design with many books that contain nothing but collections of interesting designs to help the creative process along. As your web design skills progress, even flipping through these books can be helpful in addition to a regular search for examples on the web.

3.7 REVIEW

- Some of the basic elements of design are line, shape, space, and texture.
- Line is used for outlining objects, and has direction. The direction of a line—horizontal, vertical, and diagonal—can convey meaning.
- Shape can be geometric (circles, squares, and triangles), or organic.
- Positive and negative space describe the foreground and background of the image respectively.
- Visual texture describes the look and feel of an image.

- Some of the basic principles of design are movement, balance, rhythm, and emphasis.
- Movement is the principle of how motion can be produced in a static image.
- Balance, symmetric or asymmetric, is determined by the visual weight of the elements in the image.
- Rhythm is how elements regularly repeat to form patterns in an image.
- Emphasis describes the way that certain elements are made to stand out by changing their shape, color, weight, value, or position.

⁙ 3.8 QUESTIONS

1. Define the following terms:
   a. Line
   b. Positive space
   c. Negative space
   d. Movement
   e. Shape
   f. Emphasis
   g. Texture
   h. Rhythm
   i. Balance
   j. Visual weight

2. Fill in the blank:
   a. When a page has many elements on one side and very few on the other, it has an asymmetric _____.
   b. The background of an image is called _____ _____.
   c. Repeating elements in a recognizable pattern is called _____.
   d. Interrupting a pattern by a change in shape, color, or positioning is used to create _____.
   e. Circles and squares are two examples of _____ shapes.
   f. A _____ connects two points.
   g. A green pepper shape, as shown in figure 3.7 has a/an _____ shape.
   h. The primary visual element of the Mondrian painting, "Composition with Red, Yellow and Blue," is _____.
   i. In figure 3.ex1, _____, _____, and _____ are being used to create _____.

Figure 3. ex1

j. In figure 3.ex2, color is used to indicate _____.

Figure 3. ex2

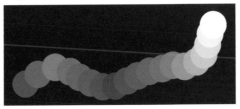

3. True or false:
   a. Line can be used to create shape.
   b. Balance refers to a design with the same number of elements on each side of the image.
   c. When determining balance, the following shapes in figure 3.ex3 have the same visual weight:

   Figure 3. ex3

   d. Both elements in figure 3.ex3 are primary shape elements (as opposed to line).
   e. In figure 3.ex3, there is no white in the positive space.
   f. The principle of movement describes how motion is suggested in an image.
   g. Negative space does not have shape.
   h. For a series of repeated elements to have rhythm, they do not necessarily need to be equally spaced.
   i. The formatting of text elements on a page can be used to indicate shape, line, or movement.
   j. In order for an element to be emphasized, it must be different in at least two ways from the surrounding elements. For example, in figure 3.8, the circle is emphasized because of a shape and color difference. If there were only one difference—say the circle were black like the squares—then it would not be proper to say that the circle is being emphasized.

4. List the three websites you use most often. Analyze them according to the principles and elements described here.
   a. Is there a coherent graphic design?
   b. Have the designers paid attention to things like balance, emphasis, and rhythm?
   c. Does the page appear chaotic, or organized and stable?

5. Search the web and find two pages that are excellent examples of graphic design. Describe the design of each in terms of the concepts presented in this chapter.

6. What is added to a design by using an asymmetric balance or irregular rhythm? What might those features create compared to a balanced design or one with regular rhythm?

7. If you were making a website that was supposed to be soothing and calming to the viewer, how would you use the following design features:

   a. Line—what direction or types of lines would you use and why?

   b. Color—what color schema would you use and why?

   c. Rhythm—what type of rhythm would you use and why?

8. In this chapter we saw optical illusions in the section on movement and in the image from M.C. Escher which confused positive and negative space. What problems are presented optical illusion based web designs. Can you think of a place in a web page or site where an optical illusion might be used effectively as a design element?

3.9 EXERCISES

1. For each of the items in Question 1, create a drawing that illustrates each. For example, a drawing like figure 3.8 would illustrate a change in rhythm.

2. Get an ad-heavy magazine. Bridal and fashion magazines are particularly useful for this exercise.

   a. Choose several "good" ads and several "bad" ads (just based on your opinion of their appearance).

   b. For each, describe the elements and principles of design used there.

   c. If there is a color schema used, identify it and the major color components.

   d. Cut apart the "bad" ads into their individual elements, and rearrange them on a sheet of paper to redesign the ad in a better way. Justify your redesign.

3. Select an organization, company, or topic as the subject of a hypothetical website (like the In A Can site in these examples). Using pen and paper or graphics software, sketch designs for your site's homepage that have to the following design features:

   a. Symmetric balance and regular rhythm using line as the primary element.

   b. Create movement in the page with organic shapes as the main element.

   c. Heavily emphasize the difference between positive and negative space using geometric shapes with asymmetric balance.

   d. Emphasize two different elements in any way (color, shape, balance, etc). Use a heavy texture as a strong element in the design.

4. Create a web page that uses background images to create texture. Use two types of texture. Consider the following example that has a checked pattern in the far background, and a light swirling shape directly behind the text.

Figure 3.ex4: A website with a close-up of background textures

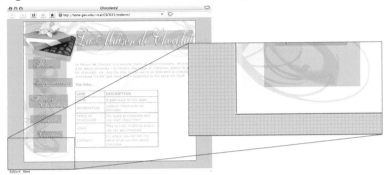

5. Project A: Consider the elements and their composition as discussed in this chapter. Choose which dominant elements you want to use in your website for Project A.

   a. Design images for navigation that use the visual elements you have chosen. Work within the color schema you designed in chapter 2.

   b. Assemble a template page that has the main navigational elements, background images, titles, and other elements that will appear on every page. Consider adding a background image to add texture while preserving readability (recall the discussion about backgrounds in chapter 2).

   c. Decide how the text for each page should be positioned. Will it be in blocks to echo shapes in the page? Will it echo movement or line within the page? Consider this placement as you make a general decision about how the text will fit into the template.

   d. Once the template is complete, carry the design through to each of the pages you have previously made. Format the text content according to the design you have chosen.

APPENDIX A: HTML COLOR REFERENCE

∴ A.1 HTML STANDARD COLOR NAMES

The following color names are defined as part of the HTML standard. There are many other color names in use, but they are not part of the standard and thus are not supported the same way in all browsers.

Color Name	Hexadecimal Code	Color
Black	#000000	
Green	#008000	
Silver	#C0C0C0	
Lime	#00FF00	
Gray	#808080	
Olive	#808000	
White	#FFFFFF	
Yellow	#FFFF00	

Color Name	Hexadecimal Code	Color
Maroon	#800000	
Navy	#000080	
Red	#FF0000	
Blue	#0000FF	
Purple	#800080	
Teal	#008080	
Fuchsia	#FF00FF	
Aqua	#00FFFF	

∴ A.2 WEB SAFE COLORS

The following table shows the hexadecimal codes and color swatches for the 216 web safe colors. Note that all of the standard color names above are not part of the web safe palate.

Hexadecimal Code	Color	Hexadecimal Code	Color	Hexadecimal Code	Color
#FFFFFF		#CCFFFF		#99FFFF	
#FFFFCC		#CCFFCC		#99FFCC	
#FFFF99		#CCFF99		#99FF99	
#FFFF66		#CCFF66		#99FF66	
#FFFF33		#CCFF33		#99FF33	
#FFFF00		#CCFF00		#99FF00	
#FFCCFF		#CCCCFF		#99CCFF	
#FFCCCC		#CCCCCC		#99CCCC	
#FFCC99		#CCCC99		#99CC99	
#FFCC66		#CCCC66		#99CC66	

Table continued on next pages

A-1

⠿ A.2 WEB SAFE COLORS CONTINUED

Hexadecimal Code	Color	Hexadecimal Code	Color	Hexadecimal Code	Color
#FFCC33		#CCCC33		#99CC33	
#FFCC00		#CCCC00		#99CC00	
#FF99FF		#CC99FF		#9999FF	
#FF99CC		#CC99CC		#9999CC	
#FF9999		#CC9999		#999999	
#FF9966		#CC9966		#999966	
#FF9933		#CC9933		#999933	
#FF9900		#CC9900		#999900	
#FF66FF		#CC66FF		#9966FF	
#FF66CC		#CC66CC		#9966CC	
#FF6699		#CC6699		#996699	
#FF6666		#CC6666		#996666	
#FF6633		#CC6633		#996633	
#FF6600		#CC6600		#996600	
#FF33FF		#CC33FF		#9933FF	
#FF33CC		#CC33CC		#9933CC	
#FF3399		#CC3399		#993399	
#FF3366		#CC3366		#993366	
#FF3333		#CC3333		#993333	
#FF3300		#CC3300		#993300	
#FF00FF		#CC00FF		#9900FF	
#FF00CC		#CC00CC		#9900CC	
#FF0099		#CC0099		#990099	
#FF0066		#CC0066		#990066	
#FF0033		#CC0033		#990033	
#FF0000		#CC0000		#990000	
#66FFFF		#33FFFF		#00FFFF	
#66FFCC		#33FFCC		#00FFCC	
#66FF99		#33FF99		#00FF99	
#66FF66		#33FF66		#00FF66	
#66FF33		#33FF33		#00FF33	

⁚⁚ **A.2** WEB SAFE COLORS CONTINUED

Hexadecimal Code	Color	Hexadecimal Code	Color	Hexadecimal Code	Color
#66FF00		#33FF00		#00FF00	
#66CCFF		#33CCFF		#00CCFF	
#66CCCC		#33CCCC		#00CCCC	
#66CC99		#33CC99		#00CC99	
#66CC66		#33CC66		#00CC66	
#66CC33		#33CC33		#00CC33	
#66CC00		#33CC00		#00CC00	
#6699FF		#3399FF		#0099FF	
#6699CC		#3399CC		#0099CC	
#669999		#339999		#009999	
#669966		#339966		#009966	
#669933		#339933		#009933	
#669900		#339900		#009900	
#6666FF		#3366FF		#0066FF	
#6666CC		#3366CC		#0066CC	
#666699		#336699		#006699	
#666666		#336666		#006666	
#666633		#336633		#006633	
#666600		#336600		#006600	
#6633FF		#3333FF		#0033FF	
#6633CC		#3333CC		#0033CC	
#663399		#333399		#003399	
#663366		#333366		#003366	
#663333		#333333		#003333	
#663300		#333300		#003300	
#6600FF		#3300FF		#0000FF	
#6600CC		#3300CC		#0000CC	
#660099		#330099		#000099	
#660066		#330066		#000066	
#660033		#330033		#000033	
#660000		#330000		#000000	

❝APPENDIX B: ARTWORKS

▼ Nude Descending a Staircase
Marcel Duchamp

© 2004 Artists Rights Society (ARS)
New York / ADAGP, Paris / Succession Marcel Duchamp

▼ Composition with Red, Yellow
and Blue, 1927
Oil on Canvas, 49.5 x 49.5cm
Piet Mondrian

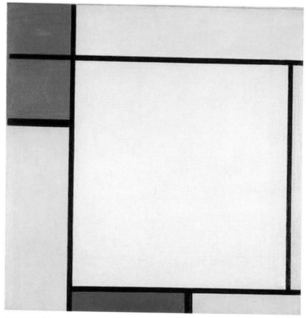

▼ Plane Filling II
M.C. Escher

INDEX

NOTES

Fairleigh Dickinson University Library
Teaneck, New Jersey

T001-15M
11-8-02